The Bliss Delusion Tango

The Bliss Delusion Tango

Poems

Maria-Cristina Necula

Library of Congress Control Number:		2009908812
ISBN:	Hardcover	978-1-4415-6922-6
	Softcover	978-1-4415-6921-9

To order additional copies of this book, contact:
Xlibris Corporation
1-888-795-4274
www.Xlibris.com
Orders@Xlibris.com
68194

Contents

Foreword

The Bliss Delusion Tango is the second published collection of Maria-Cristina Necula's poems, which are beautiful windows into her soul. They are vibrant and rich with a divine and delicious tension between classical form and contemporary feeling, and between unbearable sadness and ecstatic pleasure. This poet, influenced by both European and American culture, reveals to us terrible loss, wondrous discovery, love, disillusionment, faith, cynicism, heavenly joy, and hellish despair.

Using the English language as a plaything, Maria-Cristina Necula bends it to her will until its bones break, revealing the marrow of our most intense emotions. At the same time, she skillfully pays homage to traditional poetic forms and structure by using them in new ways. She bridges both the centuries and the oceans that separate her many sources of inspiration, creating her own unique voice—very much here and now, but heavy and rich with the wealth of poets of the past.

Yeshe Gyamtso
Woodstock, New York
August 2009

Entangled Particles

You and I
Deny
All sense of space

entangled particles
like misplaced articles
thousands of miles apart

The slightest alteration of my heart
echoes in you
misunderstood

but you are changed

Your every subtle modifying state
Predicts my inner fate
One second earlier than its dénouement

entangled particles
Souls spun from threads of singular consent
One Matter the Gods bent
and split in two

I and You

Fed dissonant delusions,
Vanity, and age
Like some experiment in rage

what alteration would the heart not face
for its entangled particle to mirror Love's embrace?

May 11, 2009—New York

Tribute to the Dawn of the Age of Aquarius

Beyond the magnet of the Self,
The Water-Bearer lifts the mind
Above the borders of mankind.
At dawn Aquarius is crowned,
New spheres of consciousness unbound,
Unveiling a cosmic design:
Humanity's unchartered shrine.
It is the Age of selfless light,
Reversal and blissful insight.
The Water-Bearer's paths unlace
As Soul and Universe embrace.

February 14, 2009—New York

I have a history
but I am now . . .
a blink of heart
upon the tomb of time
it is no accident
that every yesterday
dies pregnant with
tomorrow

January 14, 2009—White Plains

Ghost of the Year Award

I love your personalities,
Your fragmented normalities
and every time I go online
I feel like John Nash in a cipher shrine . . .

and as I cruise the internet,
There's one more you I haven't met . . .
My web hits talk to me in codes,
My chat room constantly implodes . . .

Or is it an obsession now?
We hate commitment anyhow,
It's easier to tie the knot,
To knot the tie, to stir the pot
Behind the mask of cyber waves
Where your heart is a shadow of all it craves.

Now you are just a lonely wave,
Brain wave, nerve wave, cyber wave,
and suddenly you are so brave,
disconnected from your real name,
from outlets of distress or shame . . .
'Cause modern love is cyber love,
No liquids in the mix,
And modern fantasies are you,
your laptop
and your heated clicks.

But my information's classified,
You've got a reason to decide,
This evening what's your state of mind:
Dr. Jekyll or Mr. Hyde?

My information's classified,
You will reveal just when you try to hide,
You will be one just as you pulverize,
You will know less after you analyze . . .

And it's all wondrously clear
The Ghost of the Year
Award goes to you . . .

December 30, 2008—White Plains

Torrents

Torrents of you
Taste of devastation
Spiced with my inclination
To stretch
Unfathomable truths

Torrents of you
Surprise me
In this millisecond
I'd labeled "waterproof"

Cut through the blackest velvet
Of cosmic nothingness
And pierce emptiness to shreds

Torrents of you
Are seeping in slow flow

Detachment is a fracture

Like an astral cascade
Of agonizing rapture
Torrents of you invade

December 6, 2008—White Plains

believe

I believe
in you
in the deep mystery
of all your shapes and forms

I hear you
within the subtlest whisper
of the wind
I see you past
the veils
of all realities

Your energy flows through me
within the flux and reflux
of your wisdom's ocean

I believe
in your eternal force
you
my illumination
and
my timeless
Love

October 22, 2008—White Plains

compass

this floating psyche has been pulverized
I anchor it through consonants and vowels
I pull my mind—the phantom ship—at bay
with ropes of words weaved
into sentences

my pen my compass

soul mind dissolved
scattering erasing shapes
deleting data
convulsions of the
Self
now searching for refuge in something
solid
calciferous
withdrawing into bones
stuffing itSelf inside tendons muscles tissues
crying "save me save me
from the emptiness out there
from the freedom out there!"

for Self is terrorized by infinity
it hides it hides
until bones ache and tendons strain and muscles cramp
and this unique mortal carcass is a shelter
of pain
self-destructing by violent longing to contain
its truth

because the eyes see
and the mind knows the familiar flashes
glimpses of past present future colliding into one
all in one instant
all consuming
all too burdensome and wondrous
responsibility to know
to see

and clinging to my pen
within the terrifying space of this limitless now
I sketch a path of term-less ink across the border
of an unchartered "me"

October 12, 2008—airplane Chicago to White Plains

It's Not

It's not
for smiles I lost before,
that I have tried
to win your love

It's not
the longing for the past
that tears me up inside

It's not
for bandaging a wounded soul,
that I have fought
to make you see
me

It's not for self-delusion
or for pride,
that I have sought
to stride
along the captivating mines
of your hypnotic signs

It's not for tricks and not for victory,
that I have weaved my mind
around this magical consuming
fantasy

It's not to play a game or act a part—
Defeat was always mine
Right from the start—
It's not to compensate
A broken heart

It's not for any reason
but one
true:
the endless love I feel for you
when you
are
you

October 4, 2008—White Plains

In the Dark

No peace tonight
For hope is carrying
A suitcase filled with sadness
And airports are jammed
With all the tears I own

Like passengers awaiting
Flights,
My tears too
Are voyagers
Boarding heartbeats
Like tiny airplanes outbound
Into this endless night,
Guided by flight controls
From far beyond
Imagination's borders.

Echoes of you—the pilots of my heartbeats . . .
For in the womb of time, your soul understood mine.

And yet this night,
Another night
Without my arms around you,
Without my eyes reflected into yours,
My every fiber's stretched past
All endurance
And sorrow coils softly 'round my faith

In the dark,
All I can whisper to my weary spirit
To crush despair's spawn
Is that
The night is always darkest before dawn.

September 26-27, 2008—White Plains

Oxygen

the air today
is rarefied and pure
as it must be
at the top of Everest
where every breath
is hungry for the next
and mortals share
the oxygen
of Gods

so it is here
atop the cyber promise
of a tender cue
that every precious particle
of oxygen
for me
is you

September 23, 2008—New York

I'd rather . . .

Hoffmann's glasses broke,
But I guard mine intact.
I'd rather write my hours
Here
Beyond fact.

I'd rather live to feel
This passion's miracle,
Such that I've never known
Than own
The reel
Of scenes considered "real."

I'd rather claim beliefs and hopes
That sanity condones,
I'd rather sing and hear unearthly tones
Than glide above the daily surface
And pretend.

The life I've known
Is at its end.

So Time brings forth
A deeper time and sense,
An unpredictable return
To innocence.

I'd rather stay right here
Unaware of *me*,
A mutant slave to poetry,
An instrument,
A complement
To cyber energy.

I'd rather get drunk on the joy
That you exist and breathe,
That somewhere there's a time
Backwards, forwards . . . no matter . . .
A time when distances will shatter
And love command supreme.

I'd rather dance that dream
Than lock my worldly days
Inside a muffled scream.

August 24, 2008—White Plains

Lualgo (L.u.a.l.Go)

At times I'd feel so trapped
Inside a box of chocolate "should"s
And melted ice cream "maybe"s
Where my doubts would court and reproduce
A million horrid babies

It was so cramped, so dark in there
That air itself would gasp for air
There was no time yet time stood still
Spinning around the same old skill
to *hide hide hide hide hide*

Until I came up with a word
A bird with letter wings
That sings
All my doors open every time
A word invented out of woe:
L.u.a.l.go
Loosen.up.and.let.go

Breaking out
Of this shell
What a pity
such a nice girl
take a pill
accommodate
catch yourself
before you hate

So much censorship in tow
What's an arrow without a bow?
Should you reap what you don't sow . . .
Lualgo
Loosen.up.and.let.go

I stood inside
A Windexed mind
But the edges of my brain
Overflow
You can't contain
the Wild
the elephant inside a shower cabin
the monkey in a conference room

We always know
When it's time to *know*
Lualgo
Loosen.up.and.let.go

A pair of jeans
A fake tattoo
Some copper in my hair
A stranger's eyes, a foreign town
It's all I need
I'm there
impulse-bare

The cork pops off
brain fizzles out
like champagne with a mission
A bath, a flood
A blood
transmission
A zoned-out intuition

The world is what you grow
Lualgo
Loosen.up.and.let.go

Define a style
Unleash a smile
But only when it's gut-born
Not torn
From lips who'd rather pout
Not placed on hips to make them doubt
Their nature
So sue me if I shout
Today I don't draw my happy face
it's not that kind of day
So what if I spent all my hours
On the pillows of the Afro Café?

I'm in the flow
Can't hold me back now, no,
it's been spreading everywhere
like fish roe
subversive undertow
Lualgo
Loosen.up.and.let.go

August 12, 2008—Salzburg, Austria

3:29

Cascades of joy and peace
Caress my soul

3:29 AM
And cosmic crystals
Return the light into its brightest colors

A myriad of waterfalls imploded overnight
Soothing the desert's vast
And burning scream
In its new skin
The snake dances in softness
To the sweet whisper of enchanted truth
And music of all spheres
Invades the subdued senses
Like kisses rich in healing and in faith
All will stands still
When the Invisible
Reveals its treasures to the pure heart

Within the labyrinth of human motivations
The spirit twists and turns until it bleeds to find
The path to that original, eternal seed of love
That blooms its miracles
When planted into truth

June 6, 2008—New York

In Bliss

If Kundalini called my name

I would not know to answer

For at last she holds

My cells

In bliss

Of deconstruction

June 6, 2008—New York

King to Queen

The pawn has reached A8 and seen
Her first millennium as Queen,
A Queen at Glamis Castle crowned
Between old Angus and Dundee,
Where Fate informs her to demand
The blessed hand
That set her free.

"Thy letters have transported me beyond
This ignorant present
And I feel now
The future in the instant." ***

*"Glamis, thou art!"*** Shakespearean scene
Haunted by spectral mysteries . . .

A wedding for all centuries
Within your halls or by the Sea?
Two windows to the secret room,
The Red Lady and her bridegroom.

Your faith grants me eternity,
Your tests call love to the North Sea
To ancient Angus and Dundee . . .

"Art thou afeared to be the same
In thine own act and valor
As thou art in desire?" ***
Lady Macbeth may grant you fire
Not for the curse ambitions bring
But for the courage of a king.

Your lasting sovereignty prove
And King to Queen in Glamis move.

*(*** Quotes from "Macbeth" by William Shakespeare)*
June 1, 2008—New York

Evening Thoughts

I think we seek out
Those who do not want us
So we can find the way
To want Ourselves.

I think we long for
Those who do not *see* us
So we can view our flaws
In unflattering light.

I think we fight for
Those who won't be fought for,
Not for the conquest
But for its possibility.

I think we back our hearts
Into tight corners
So we can dream the freedom
Of release.

I think we claim
To have forgotten danger
So we can build
The tunnels to escape.

I think we can't content
Ourselves with stillness,
So we can strive for peace
When we are chaos.

I think we own our answers.
But we won't find the questions
Until we walk beside, against, and into
One Another.

May 28, 2008—White Plains

Timely Argument

I had an argument with time

It cost me half a decade

Of counting yesterdays

But I have never spent

A second

On my cursed lament

Of living sooner than

The Chronos intent

May 27, 2008—White Plains

Return to Earth

I'm entering into my earthly phase . . .
Last night the senses all surrounded me:
"Drop anchor, woman, into Nature's soil,
Forget chimeras of a time that might exist,
Life is not fed by tasting stratospheres
And passion rarely sizzles in the abstract,
Plant your kaleidoscope of stories
Into the mud and glories
Of today,
Release the seeds of beauty from your guarded hand
Into the bloody womb of Here
And watch the blossoms of your everyday
Exceed the floating fantasies of air,
Deny Aquarius its detached lack of care,
Surrender to the Sea-Goat's earthy flair,
Return to walk the garden of delights and flaws
And switch cerebral settings to 'Pause.'"

May 23, 2008—New York

Word-Made

I had a dream that I was made of words,
From head to toe, a body built by sentences and paragraphs,
Coherent and absurd,
Entirely dependent on the letters,
For their arrangements
Rendered magic to my flesh.

If you could read me limb by limb
And cell by cell,
And every foreign term of my construction learn to spell,
You'd turn this dictionary of exhausting contradictions
Into your own encyclopedia
Of tender definitions.

May 23, 2008—White Plains

Unmask

Voracious Sir,
It is a mutual anomaly
That we both claim to be
Serious.

There is no ban on ecstasy
As long as we both play
Delirious.

"Vacate the premises" of someone's heart
Is tough
But not as rough
As cloning past desires.
For it's no longer human what inspires
Such constancy to repetition.
It's an act of indulgent attrition,
The perverse will to strive
In orbits 'round a Moon that will not jive.

Although we learn of its volcanic landscape,
Of its beauty's dependence on the sun;
We orbit 'round and 'round
And give it credit.

It's but a sterile rock that light will edit
And exalt.

It's not our fault that sometimes what we gaze upon
Reflects but not returns
The love we cradle and expect.
We're light and sound effect,
Director, actors, all
The cast and crew;
That magic show was you applauding you.

And so, shy, lusty Sir,
I ask:
'Isn't it better to remove the mask
With built-in tunnel vision and refractors?
Why not examine the true factors
Contributing to this impasse?

My point is rather crass
But faithful to my line of thought:

Let's not
Define each other by the light we give.
Let's sign our pleasure treaty
And let live.'

May 2008—White Plains

Golden Bet

Golden, golden woman
Pouring out her light
Into the corners where the night
Stole space inside my head,
Her wisdom spread
As gloriously as a summer sky.
Mother and friend,
You never end
To bridge the gaps between myself and I,
To unify
Faith and surrender in a single smile.
It's been a fascinating while,
And I am closer yet
To the most you have bet
I'll ever be:
Me.

May 2008—White Plains

Portrait

Imperfect and hypnotic,
Neurotic,
She wraps her sense of humor 'round her neck
Like an expensive shawl.

She walks the walk of all
Those women who have bent their genes
To taste the fate of figurines
Displayed within the female Hall of Lame.

Until it came:
The knowledge of Nothing-To-Lose,
That single-handed cruise
To nowhere, out of time,
Sublime
And still.

And so it dawned on her
That God and Lucifer
Both rent apartments in her mind,
While hell and heaven here on Earth contain
The choice between autonomy and passive pain.

May 2008—White Plains

Point in Possibility?

The viral truth
Knows no antibiotic,
Lurking without bestowing
Upon stripped beliefs
Designed reliefs.

Confined by chance
To dance
Inside the mirrors of our Self-Absorb,
We move like planets
Of a jagged orb
Among commercial strategies and glossy bliss,
Our happiness a test of hit-or-miss.

My disillusioned questioner, believe:
This is no sinking ship,
This is the captain's choice,
The schizophrenic voice
Completing lacks
And outward-guided deeds,
Taming the arrows of crazed needs.

The kangaroo with its maternal pouch
Would teach hyenas how to care
If they could meet on common ground and dare
To cross the barrier of tongues and nature.

What world is this where I remember you
Before you happened?
Where words collide outside
Before they bow to truth inside?

This verbal chain of meaning and effect,
The curse of hyperactive intellect . . .
Talk, talk, talk,
And so it's talked about.
But can you do without?

Can you become a point
In self-reduction,
A needle's tip,
A tiny clip
Of self containing all?
Can you become the answer to your call,
The echo to your scream,
The characters within your dream?
Is it that you are all
Manifestations of your thought
Upon the outer world reflected?
Or is it that you give
More of yourself to possibility
Rather than claiming actuality
To furnish your headquarters
Of reality?

May 2008—White Plains

That Place

Today it hurts to write
Because It looms right there,
Elusive and essential as the air . . .

I scrape
With surgical devotion
Down to the bone marrow of notion
And when I briefly touch
The core of It
At one with pure Eternity, I'm hit
By such an awe that crushes and devours
And wipes the minutes off my slate of hours,

A paralyzing joy and dread in one,
I cannot name it but I know it well,
That Place contains both Paradise and Hell
That Place of words and fertile nudity
Where birth and death align
The corpse inside the womb,
The fetus in the tomb . . .

That Place where every microscopic dream unheard
Is born in death, word after word . . .

May 2008—White Plains

Who Can?

I can't fit in!
I can't fit in!
Said the spirit to the skin.

I can't conform!
I can't conform!
Said the rebel to the norm.

I can't relax!
I can't relax!
Said the Queen's neck to the ax.

I can't comply!
I can't comply!
Said the tongue to the white lie.

I can't resist!
I can't resist!
Said the sinner to the priest.

I can't pretend!
I can't pretend!
Said the artist to the trend.

I can't sustain!
I can't sustain!
Said the neuron to the pain.

I can't be sold!
I can't be sold
Said the honor to the gold.

I can't forget!
I can't forget!
Said the heartache to regret.

I can't control!
I can't control!
Said the star to the black hole.

I can't refuse!
I can't refuse!
Said the Yenta to the news.

I can't destroy!
I can't destroy!
Said the fairy to the toy.

I can't escape!
I can't escape!
Said the man's genes to the ape.

I can't command!
I can't command!
Said the hourglass to the sand.

I can't correct!
I can't correct!
Said the cause to the effect.

I can't reply!
I can't reply!
Said the echo to the cry.

I can't return!
I can't return!
Said the ashes to the urn.

I can't say 'no'!
I can't say 'no'!
Said the mistress to her glow.

I can't be wise!
I can't be wise!
Said the longing to the eyes.

I can't be caught!
I can't be caught!
Said the instinct to the thought.

I can't be me!
I can't be me!
Said I to my memory.

May 2008—White Plains

The Fish and the Bird

it's a lonely, lonely way to pair up
it's a guaranteed assumptions' flare-up
You can't tell the butterfly to fly in a straight line
I can't make Your taste buds turn champagne into red wine

if the Fish will love the Bird, they'll never meet at sea
and the sky can cry all day, and still We'll never be
but a slow disaster in the making
but an oven filled with tempers baking
oil and water, salt and sugar blending
for each word of love, ten words offending

it's a wild guessing game to understand
it's a highway to compassion, built on moving sand
You can't blame the Air for never mirroring the ground
I can't place Your undertones in my repertoire of sound

if the Bird will love the Fish, they'll never meet in flight
and the sea can boil and bubble, still We claim no right
but this lifelong riddle by request
My "Da Vinci Code", Your Puppet Quest

March 8, 2008—White Plains

No More

No darkness and no pain
No ciphers and no codes
No Lunar nodes

No more

The Door
is old and wrong

The dune
The lying Moon
The split
The double hit
Have lost
The force to cost
My soul
Its precious stones

The clones
Are sterile
And deprived

I have arrived
Beyond the arrows
Of my deep contempt
Unkempt
Unhinged
But true
To all I knew
Maintaining Me intact

The pact
Is dead

My head
No longer needs to scream
The ego and the dream

My heart
No longer claims to feel
Unreal

My body and my skin
My sorrow and my name
No longer intertwine
In shame

No more

The air
Is cold and stale
Behind the writing wall
I fall
Prey to my errant call

Within the cage
I age
Illogical and unconcerned
For all I've earned
In past grief
And belief

No more

The Door
Exploded into scars
Like rusty stars
Upon my soul's uncensored vault
No fault
No tears
No "why"s

But wisdom's eyes
On all that's lost and loved
On all that's bled and hoped
On all that's torn and wailed
On all that's blessed and failed

Here is my truth

I stand inside
Of one heart
Of one mind
Of one Self, of one kind
Amiss and found

Unbound

February 25, 2008—White Plains

Desert Ride

I'm riding through the desert
the sun is ripping sky
and crashing on my shoulders
like a scorching cry

it doesn't matter where I start
to count the shades of gold
I'm sold
a bargain for my untold heart

how would I trace
the promise of your silhouette
when every grain of sand is shallow
when haunted by your Islam shadow
my blood flows to the minaret
of ancestral regret

I got to the oasis
hot and blinded by the space
every corner of my mind
a portrait of your face

this spot is new
the caravans are passing through
but I cannot quench myself
beyond me and you

2008—New York

Walk My World

Is it "forever" that I see
Etched in your silent rhapsody,
Riddled with notes of crescent moons
And parakeets, and silver spoons?

Are you the clown on Stirbei Street
Where women come to pluck and greet
The lines of gossip-studded lips
Behind the gates of silver tips?

Are you the puppet on this stage,
My home, the wizard of my age?
You walk my world of "long ago"s
Without a trace of claim or cause.

What do you know of glances bare
In old University Square,
The Intercontinental lure
Above the National's allure?

Exceptional, though sought beyond
Ability to break a bond,
You lie awake besides the clock,
The surreptitious Balkan mock,

It's late, delayed, behind your snare,
The mythical rhythm and air
Of Latin blood and Slavic tricks
With Turkish delights in the mix.

You twist beyond your normal vein
When the necessity for pain
Is puzzling and spares no relief,
Except a pounding, absurd grief.

In Bucharest lay down your head,
In Bucharest you'll burn your bed,
In Bucharest, your pride is weak,
In Bucharest you hide and seek.

Surreal is this charmed domain
Beyond your mortal reach to gain,
Enigma of the fleeting flowers
That eat up all your days and hours.

You thought you came at Fortune's call.
Coincidence and know-it-all
Won't get you past the tolls of lore,
The longing rocks you to the core.

Romania with fragrant wings,
Romania where each street sings,
Romania of pulse and schemes,
Romania ensnares your dreams.

By touch and smell and sight and sound,
Your stranger's heart forever bound
Will crash against the sight of you
Condemned to face a clever coup.

You won't survive the dance, the eyes,
The veiled "yes" will hypnotize.
You long to walk my world? Begin
By shedding your omniscient skin.

September 3, 2007—Irvington, New York

Woman Rising

I lie burning
And she rises
Rises over me
Body tower
Body column
Of audacity

"Now you die
You silver dust
Gilded lily flower
Painted angel
Rustic in your power"
Time to die
Woman to woman
"Sister drop the load"

Lie in bed
Rotating longings
Look for corners
In the circle
Dress the fly
In butterfly
Wings and petal love

Lie in bed and
Count survival
One, two, three, four, five and nine
Woman of nine lives and answers
Woman live and memory die

I lie crystallized reflecting
Faces cloned
At dawn's defiance
More and more and more
I weather
Songs of misalliance

Woman rising over woman
Burning bridges of Amend
I lie soft
She dictates higher
Woman tower
Woman flower
By genetic bend

May 1, 2007—New York

The Valley of Bliss

They sway in ecstasy
as the tenderest echoes of pleasure
a moan
wailing silently
"You are not enough yourself"

They sway in slow motion
In Bliss

The Valley of Bliss

their crowns are like
artesian fountains
a burst of leaves longing upward
it's not for show
it's not on purpose

They come unto themselves
in agreement
nodding their leafy heads

Looks like they're conversing

The Valley of Bliss
is alive with
undulating chants
weaving a melody of hushed flirtation
"we're here, we're here, we're here
take us in despite your pain

you can encompass us
if you do not cling
let this beauty
flow through your soul
like a fresh brook
because you're here too
and no one knows . . ."

I look at them:
'By what power do you sway
Your whispers blooming with each breeze?'

They sway whirling their emerald crowns
Nameless kings of the valley
The Valley of Bliss
Their windy answer brings
Relief:
"We sway by the sweet power
Of your
untapped
Belief"

April 2007—Malibu, California

Winter Now

The trees
On the slanted white
Have winter fingers
Playing an invisible piano
Of collective harmonies
Curled
Beneath a cloak
Of vibrant stillness.

The trees
On the slanted white
Have winter arms
Conducting
An orchestra of delicate murmurs
Veiled
By the immobility
Of pure bliss.

The trees
On the slanted white
Bow
Towards those who care
To know
What they have always known
Since the start of the
Performance:

This very moment
In its endless flow
Of immaculate falling pearls
Is a portrait of tranquil purity
By a master painter
Commissioned
By this very moment's
Self-importance.

The Now of now
Wanted to introduce itself
To Eternity,
Carefully adorned
In filigree of white and unvoiced music
For fear that the passers-by
Would pass it by.

Like so many other "Now"s,
This Now is elegantly
Yearning
For immortality.

February 26, 2007—Kensico Dam, New York

Take Me There Once More

(For Mark Patnode's paintings of Bulgaria)

In a corner of the world,
Beauty and spirit unfurled,
By the grace of Nature's rite,
Wrapped my soul in endless light.

Drops of blue and green and white,
Kiss away the magic night,
Sunrise song and sunset glow,
Devil's Bridge and river's flow.

I spent a summer in your arms,
Breathing in your subtle charms,
In simple beauty, deep and kind,
You shaped the landscape of my mind.

I knew your colors one by one,
I stood beneath your glorious sun,
I felt the wonder born to last,
Captured whispers of your past.

Touched by your sky,
Let my soul begin to fly
With your ancient lullaby,
Let me feel your colors sway,
And one day,
I'll carry you on my way.

2007—White Plains

Christmas Delirium or The Tree, The Bible, and The Box

Under the fragrant Tree
I opened up the Box
Where Christmas lies within a diagram of regulated motions
Wherein the hand that feeds is but the hand that robs.

The sacramental factions of thieves and relat(h)ieves
Do shake the holy altars
Smeared in coal and blood.
May circumstances change
While mud flows in the kitchens
Upon these soldiers toiling
"For better and for worse."

The voice of carols heralds
Permission to sustain
The chains of absolution.
It's Christmas bait and tainted angels
At the door,
And underneath the mistletoe
The witches brew their sloth.

Salvation comes by dictum
Of all revered strangers
Whose lives render the portrait
Of bliss and home-made broth.

Where art thou, definition
Of home and sweet morality,
The comfort of hereafter and evermore forever?

Where is the snug contentment
Of futures well-projected
On frail cerebral screens?
And envelopes which hold
Numbers,
And magazines,
Newspapers neatly folded,
Crisp as the lively horrors
Nestled among their pages like vipers
Spewing ink.

Upon my head, the light,
His birth, His agony . . .
The avalanche of shame
Determined by false prophets
To chastise our short-lived
Spawns of free-form courage.

He was the great example,
The Truth, the Myth,
The Love

Robbed through idolatry contrived
By vagabonds of faith
Who stick their restless tongues
Under the sacred robes
To offer jolts of *paradism*
And enchanted flesh.

Take Christmas in a Box, a Bible
And a Tree.
It's lurking all around you, me . . .
The I, the You,
the One,
the only One it would not be . . .

And Nature
Will eternally condemn her children
For charity and compassion
Consigned to just one day
And holy pilgrimages to the mall—
Lost echoes of Her massacred abundance . . .

All the snowflakes of Antarctica
Will not sweeten this little hand
Waving at the window
On top of windows bathed in lights
To hide the night upon the Tree,
The Bible
And the Box.

Pandora, are you lost?
Among which constellations do you wander
Holding Orion's mighty hand?
For if you will not return,
The Tree, the Bible, and the Box
Will lie eternally in the dust of Calvary
And you will wail in agony
Over the ashes of philosophers,
And Shamans
Who knew Him in His lost years . . .

Lured into India, like Alexander,
He carved His thoughts upon the Tree
Where young Siddhartha dashed
The world
To find the jewels
Of Reality.

While rambling mouths and tortured hearts
Color the planet in shades of grey,
It's dark beneath the fragrant Christmas Tree.
The Bible's in the Box
Wrapped up in ribbons and glitter,
Words linger bitter,
Swirling among the garlands . . .
Whispers of what has always been unsaid,
The sorrows of the dead,
Injustices and unhealed wounds
Repeated evermore.

Step through the open door
While eggnog flows along rivers of alcohol,
It's Christmas after all.

December 25, 2006—New York